MYSTIFYING
LOGIC
PUZZLES

Norman D. Willis

Sterling Publishing Co., Inc.
New York

Books by Norman D. Willis

Amazing Logic Puzzles (1994)
Tricky Logic Puzzles (1995)
False Logic Puzzles (1997)
Challenging False Logic Puzzles (1997)
Mystifying Logic Puzzles (1998)

Edited by Claire Bazinet

Library of Congress Cataloging-in-Publication Data Available

10 9 8 7 6 5 4 3 2 1

Published by Sterling Publishing Company, Inc.
387 Park Avenue South, New York, N.Y. 10016
© 1998 by Norman D. Willis
Distributed in Canada by Sterling Publishing
C/o Canadian Manda Group, One Atlantic Avenue, Suite 105
Toronto, Ontario, Canada M6K 3E7
Distributed in Great Britain and Europe by Cassell PLC
Wellington House, 125 Strand, London WC2R 0BB, England
Distributed in Australia by Capricorn Link (Australia) Pty Ltd.
P.O. Box 6651, Baulkham Hills, Business Centre, NSW 2153, Australia
Manufactured in the United States of America

Sterling ISBN 0-8069-9721-4

CONTENTS

Before You Begin

Solving logic puzzles is challenging and enjoyable, as well as worthwhile. They will not necessarily expand your knowledge, but if approached conscientiously, they can help to develop your mental power. The puzzles involve formal logic requiring deductive reasoning based on given statements or propositions—and they will stretch your ability to successfully exercise reasoned trial and error and analyze alternatives.

One key is to resist turning to the solution for a given puzzle—until you believe you have solved the puzzle, or until you are convinced you have given it your very best effort. Finally, if you do need to turn to the answer, review the considerations leading to the solution so that you will become familiar with the approach and can use it to solve other puzzles of the same type.

Within this book are six puzzle sections. Each contains a different type of logic puzzle, and in each section the puzzles are organized by level of difficulty beginning with the least difficult and progressing to the most difficult. They are graded as follows: Those puzzles identified by one asterisk (*) are challenging yet solvable by the reader who approaches them conscientiously. Those identified by two asterisks (**) are intended to be solved by experienced logic puzzle solvers. The most difficult puzzles, identified by three asterisks (***), will be solved only by the most expert solvers.

For most puzzles, diagrams will be helpful in testing alternatives and forming conclusions. You will find suggested diagrams in both the Hints and Solutions sections of the book.

In all the logic puzzles in this book, characters with male-sounding names are male, and those with female-sounding names are female. You'll never encounter a female Lancelot or a male Mary.

—1—

Prince Tal's Adventures

The adventures of Prince Tal take place in a faraway kingdom at a distant time. Prince Tal encounters the ferocious beasts, giants, and enchantresses that abound in that land.

The puzzles in this section contain assumptions, only some of which will lead you to the correct solutions. The challenge is to determine which assumptions are valid and which are invalid.

P1-1 Educational Accomplishments*

Even though noblemen of the kingdom spent considerable time seeking adventures, education was not neglected. Prince Tal excelled in one area of his education and did especially well in another. From the following statements, determine in which subject Prince Tal excelled and in which second subject he did especially well.

1. If Prince Tal excelled in chivalry, he did especially well in horsemanship.
2. If Prince Tal excelled in horsemanship, he did especially well in fencing.
3. If Prince Tal did especially well in horsemanship, he excelled in fencing.
4. If Prince Tal excelled in fencing, he did especially well in chivalry.

5. If Prince Tal did especially well in chivalry, he excelled in horsemanship.

(Hints on page 41)
(Solution on page 53)

P1-2 Battles with Dragons*

For noblemen to do battle with dragons was considered the ultimate adventure. Sir Aard, Sir Bolbo, and Sir Delfo have each had a successful encounter with one or two dragons. Among the three noblemen, they encountered a total of five dragons: Biter, Black Heart, Dante, Flame Thrower, and Old Smoky. No dragon was encountered by more than one nobleman. Consider the following statements:

1. If Sir Aard encountered Dante, then Sir Delfo did not encounter Flame Thrower.
2. If Sir Aard did not encounter both Biter and Black Heart, then Sir Bolbo encountered Flame Thrower and Sir Delfo encountered Old Smoky.
3. If Sir Delfo encountered Black Heart, then Sir Aard encountered Dante.
4. If Sir Bolbo did not encounter both Dante and Biter, then Sir Delfo encountered Flame Thrower and Sir Aard encountered Black Heart.
5. Flame Thrower and Dante were not encountered by the same nobleman.
6. If Sir Delfo did not encounter both Black Heart and Flame Thrower, then Sir Aard encountered Biter and Sir Bolbo encountered Old Smoky.

Which noblemen encountered which dragons?

(Hints on page 41)
(Solution on pages 53–54)

P1-3 Who Tilted with Whom?*

It was the custom for noblemen to practice tilting when there were no pressing adventures. One afternoon, Sir Aard, Sir Bolbo, Sir Delfo, Sir Gath, Sir Keln, and Prince Tal paired off for this exercise into three matches. Consider the following statements:

1. If either Prince Tal or Sir Aard tilted with Sir Keln, then Sir Bolbo tilted with Sir Gath.
2. If Sir Gath tilted with Prince Tal, then Sir Keln tilted with Sir Delfo.
3. If Prince Tal tilted with Sir Delfo, Sir Keln tilted with Sir Gath.
4. If Sir Gath tilted with Sir Bolbo, Sir Delfo tilted with Prince Tal.
5. If Prince Tal tilted with Sir Aard, then Sir Bolbo tilted with Sir Gath.
6. If Sir Gath tilted with Sir Keln, then Prince Tal tilted with Sir Aard.
7. If Prince Tal tilted with Sir Bolbo, then Sir Keln tilted with Sir Aard.

Who tilted with whom?

(Hints on pages 41–42)
(Solution on pages 54–55)

P1-4 Encounter with the Fearsome Beast*

The Fearsome Beast, whose head was like that of a lion and whose hair was black and shaggy, was said to be as big as an elephant and faster than a deer. Few had ever seen it, but the beast reportedly had been observed in a remote area of the kingdom. Prince Tal and his three comrades, Sir Aard, Sir Bolbo, and Sir Delfo, were determined to confront the elusive monster. To this end, they set out in the search.

They encountered the monster, but at the first sight of the beast, their horses reared, threw two of the riders, and bolted for distant parts. One of the two thrown noblemen quickly climbed a tree, while the other was left prostrate on the ground, momentarily stunned. The Fearsome Beast jumped over the fallen nobleman and quickly departed.

From the following statements determine which nobleman was prostrate on the ground, which one climbed a tree, and which two were not unhorsed.

1. If Sir Bolbo climbed a tree, then Sir Delfo and Prince Tal were not thrown.
2. If Sir Delfo climbed a tree, then Sir Aard and Prince Tal were not thrown.
3. If Sir Aard was prostrate on the ground, then Prince Tal and Sir Bolbo were not thrown.
4. If Sir Aard was not thrown, then Sir Bolbo was not thrown, and Sir Delfo was prostrate on the ground.
5. If Prince Tal did not climb a tree, then either Sir Bolbo or Sir Delfo climbed a tree.
6. If Sir Bolbo was prostrate on the ground, then Prince Tal and Sir Delfo were not thrown.

(Hints on page 42)
(Solution on pages 55–56)

P1-5 Strange Creatures**

Strange creatures are occasionally seen in the kingdom and different kinds have been seen by different inhabitants. Given the following statements, can you determine which

of Prince Tal and his four fellow noblemen saw which kind
of creature? (No two saw the same kind of creature.)

1. If Sir Bolbo saw a monoceros, then Sir Delfo saw a
   satyr.
2. If Sir Bolbo saw a bonnacon, then Prince Tal saw a
   monoceros.
3. If Sir Keln did not see a leucrota, then Sir Aard saw a
   satyr.
4. If either Sir Bolbo or Sir Aard saw a basilisk, then Sir
   Delfo did not see a monoceros.
5. If Prince Tal saw a bonnacon, then Sir Aard saw a
   basilisk.
6. If Prince Tal saw a monoceros, then Sir Delfo saw a
   leucrota.
7. If Sir Delfo did not see a basilisk, then he saw a monoceros.
8. If Sir Delfo did not see a satyr, then Sir Bolbo did not
   see a leucrota.

(Hints on page 42)
(Solution on page 57)

P1-6 Prince Tal and the Enchantress**

As a knight-errant, Prince Tal traveled the kingdom in
search of adventure. He frequently relied on hospitality in
the castles, abbeys, and hermitages along his way. One
evening he was invited into a strange castle that, unbe-
knownst to Prince Tal, was inhabited by an enchantress
who cast a sleeping spell on him. When Prince Tal awoke,
he found himself in the castle dungeon, where he was held
for ransom.

After he was ultimately released, Prince Tal, still suffering some aftereffects of the sleep-inducing spell, had difficulty recalling how long he had been imprisoned, or how he had been freed. He could not remember whether his fellow noblemen had stormed the castle and released him, whether he had broken the dungeon door and escaped, whether the dungeon keeper (who was a loyal subject of the king) had left the dungeon door open for him, or whether the ransom had been paid.

Based on the following statements, can you clarify the outcome of Prince Tal's misadventure?

1. If the noblemen stormed the castle or the dungeon keeper left the door open, then Prince Tal was imprisoned for one day or three days.
2. If Prince Tal's imprisonment was for one day or one week, then he broke the dungeon door or the noblemen stormed the castle.
3. If Prince Tal's imprisonment was neither for three days nor for one week, then the dungeon keeper didn't leave the door open nor was the ransom paid.
4. If he broke the dungeon door or the ransom was paid, then Prince Tal was imprisoned for one week or two weeks.
5. If he did not break the door and the ransom was not paid, then Prince Tal was imprisoned for three days or the dungeon keeper left the door open.
6. If Prince Tal's imprisonment was not for one day or two weeks, then he did not break the dungeon door and the castle was not stormed.
7. If Prince Tal's imprisonment was for three days or two weeks, then the dungeon keeper left the door open or the ransom was paid.

(Hints on pages 42–43)
(Solution on page 58)

P1-7 To the Rescue***

Rescuing fair damsels in distress was an important responsibility of Prince Tal and his fellow noblemen. A total of six maidens were rescued by five noblemen. Based on the following statements, determine which damsels were rescued by which noblemen.

1. If Sir Keln rescued either Maid Marion or Maid Mary, then Sir Aard rescued either Maid Muriel or Maid Marie.
2. If Prince Tal rescued either Maid Matilda or Maid Marie, then Sir Bolbo rescued either Maid Mary or Maid Marion.
3. If Prince Tal rescued either Maid Mary or Maid Morgana, then Sir Bolbo rescued either Maid Matilda or Maid Marion.
4. If Sir Bolbo rescued either Maid Mary or Maid Marie, then Sir Keln rescued either Maid Matilda or Maid Morgana.
5. If Sir Aard rescued either Maid Muriel or Maid Marie, then Prince Tal rescued either Maid Mary or Maid Morgana.
6. If Sir Keln did not rescue either Maid Marion or Maid Mary, then Sir Aard rescued Maid Marion, unless he rescued Maid Muriel.
7. If Sir Bolbo rescued either Maid Marion or Maid Matilda, then Sir Delfo rescued both Maid Muriel and Maid Marie.
8. If Sir Aard did not rescue Maid Marie, then Prince Tal rescued Maid Marion, unless he rescued both Maid Matilda and Maid Muriel.

(Hints on page 43)

(Solution on pages 58–59)

P1-8 Prince Tal's Encounters with Four Dragons***

Among the dragons that Prince Tal has encountered, four were especially ferocious and challenging: Dante breathed plumes of flame 50 feet long (or so it seemed), Quicksilver could fly as fast as sound (or so it seemed), Vesuvius was as large as a mountain (or so it appeared), and Meduso was capable of turning to stone anyone who looked him directly in the eye (Prince Tal fought this dragon using his peripheral vision).

None of the confrontations with these four dragons was conclusive. In one case, Prince Tal's fellow noblemen arrived in time to save him. In another case, just before being overwhelmed, Prince Tal feigned death until the dragon departed. At another time, the dragon quit after developing an uncontrollable coughing fit from inhaling too much smoke (a common affliction among dragons). In another case, Prince Tal forgot his shield and had to leave without actually fighting.

From the following statements, determine the order in which Prince Tal encountered the four dragons, and what the outcome was in each case.

1. If Vesuvius was not the second or third dragon encountered, then Prince Tal's fellow noblemen arrived in time to save him during this confrontation.
2. If the first encounter was with the dragon Dante, then the fourth encounter was with the dragon Meduso.
3. If Prince Tal did not feign death during the fourth encounter, then the fourth confrontation was not with the dragon Dante.
4. If Prince Tal's fellow noblemen arrived in time to save

him during the first encounter, then the first encounter was with the dragon Quicksilver.

5. If the second encounter was with the dragon Dante, then Prince Tal's fellow noblemen arrived in time to save him.

6. If Prince Tal feigned death in his confrontation with the dragon Meduso, then it happened during the third encounter.

7. If Prince Tal's second confrontation was with Quicksilver or Vesuvius, then the dragon suffered a coughing fit during this encounter.

8. Prince Tal did not forget his shield during the first and third encounters, unless he feigned death during the second encounter.

(Hints on page 43)

(Solution on pages 60–61)

—2—

Dragons of Lidd and Wonk

There are few dragons in the kingdom of Lidd, and they have been put on the endangered species list.

Dragons are of two types. Some have reasoned that devouring domestic animals and their owners is, in the long run, not healthy for dragons. They are known as rationals. Some dragons, on the other hand, are reluctant to give up their traditional ways, nor do they fear humans. They are known as predators. The King has decreed that rational dragons shall be protected. Knights caught slaying a rational dragon are dealt with severely.

In addition to being rationals or predators, dragons in Lidd are of two different colors related to their veracity. Gray rational dragons always tell the truth; red rationals always lie. Red predators always tell the truth; gray predators always lie.

There is something appealing to a dragon about being in a land in which knights are not constantly trying to build their reputations by slaying them. It was not surprising, therefore, that the blue dragons from the adjacent land of Wonk began appearing in the kingdom of Lidd. Blue dragons are rationals or predators, but they all lie.

To tell if a dragon is protected, it would help to know its color. However, there is an affliction endemic to humans in Lidd: they are color blind. To them, all dragons look gray.

P2-1 One Dragon*

A dragon is approached by a knight looking for adventure. The dragon, asked his color and type, responds as follows:

Dragon: I am either blue or gray.

What type is the dragon?

(Hints on page 44)
(Solution on page 61)

P2-2 Two Dragons*

Two armed knights confront two dragons, each of which is asked his color and type. Their answers follow:

A. 1. I am from Wonk.
   2. B and I are both predators.
B. 1. A is not from Wonk, but I am.
   2. I am a rational.

What color and type are each dragon?

(Hints on page 44)
(Solution on page 62)

P2-3 Three Dragons*

A knight in armor cautiously approaches three dragons, who offer the following information:

A. 1. C is from Wonk.
   2. I am not a red predator.
B. 1. A is from Wonk.
   2. A and C are both rationals.
C. 1. B is from Wonk.
   2. B is a predator.

What are the color and type of each dragon?

(Hints on page 44)
(Solution on pages 62–63)

P2-4 Two Are from Wonk*

A knight confronts three dragons, exactly two of which are known to be blue dragons from Wonk, and asks each his color and type. Their answers follow:

A. 1. B is from Wonk.
   2. I am a rational.
B. 1. C is from Wonk.
   2. I am a rational.
C.   I am a rational.

What color and type are each dragon?

(Hints on page 44)
(Solution on page 63)

P2-5 One Dragon from Wonk*

Three dragons, exactly one of which is blue, provide the following information:

A. 1. C is a gray rational.
   2. I am a gray rational.
B. 1. A is a predator.
   2. A is blue.
   3. I am a rational.
C. 1. A is not gray.
   2. B is from Wonk.

What color and type are each dragon?

(Hints on page 44)
(Solution on pages 63–64)

P2-6 At Least One from Wonk*

The knights of Lidd are seeing more blue dragons than usual. Four knights encounter four dragons, at least one of which is blue, and ask about their colors and types. The dragons' statements follow:

A. 1. I am either a gray predator or a red rational.
   2. B is red.
B. 1. A and I are both rationals.
   2. C is a red predator.
   3. I am gray.
C. 1. I am not gray.
   2. I am a rational.
   3. B is a predator.
D. 1. C and I are both predators.
   2. I am red.
   3. A and B are both blue.

What are the color and type of each dragon?

(Hints on page 44)
(Solution on pages 64–65)

P2-7 Three Dragons Again*

A lone knight nervously approaches three dragons, at least one of which is from Wonk. They volunteer the following information:

A. 1. I am either red or gray.
   2. C and I are the same color.
B. 1. A is not red.
   2. C is blue.
C. 1. A's statements are false.
   2. B is not a rational.

What color and type are each dragon?

(Hints on page 44)
(Solution on page 65)

P2-8 How Many Are Protected?**

A knight looking for a dragon to slay confronts three. He asks each about his color and type. Their answers follow:

A. 1. I am gray.
   2. We three are protected by the King's decree.
   3. C is red.
B. 1. I am not protected by the King's decree.
   2. C is gray.
C. 1. A and I are not the same type.
   2. A is red.
   3. B is a rational.

What color and type are each dragon?

(Hints on pages 44–45)
(Solution on page 66)

P2-9 Who Speaks for Whom?**

Three dragons respond to a very wary knight as follows:

A. 1. If asked, B would claim that C is a predator.
   2. I am gray.
   3. B is a rational.
B. 1. If asked, C would claim that A is a rational.
   2. C is red.
C. 1. If asked, A would claim that B is red.
   2. A is gray.

What color and type are each dragon?

(Hints on page 45)
(Solution on page 67)

—3—

The Trials of Xanthius

Among the ancient Greeks, the people of Athens led all others in their mental acuity. The gods created a series of trials to test the Athenians' reasoning ability, as well as their courage (and perhaps to amuse themselves). As an incentive, they provided a fabulous treasure to be won by whoever was successful in passing every trial.

The trials involved following a path through a dense forest, across a large savanna, and up a tall mountain, with choices to be made at seven points. There was to be no turning back once the challenge was accepted, and no retracing of steps at any time. Dire consequences awaited a challenger who made an incorrect judgment.

No citizen of Athens desired to accept the risk until Xanthius, a young student of Socrates, accepted the challenge.

P3-1 The First Trial*

Hardly had Xanthius entered the forest on the designated path, when it branched into two. He was told that this was the first trial and that one way led to the second trial, while the other led near the domain of a giant serpent, for which he would undoubtedly become a meal. A sign at each path gave instruction.

However, Xanthius was informed that at least one of the signs was false. The signs read as follows:

A
```
This path leads
to the serpent.
```

B
```
The sign at
path A is true.
```

Which path is the one Xanthius should follow?

(Hints on page 45)
(Solution on page 68)

P3-2 The Second Trial*

Xanthius chose the correct path and, after proceeding into the forest for some time, he came to a branching of the path into three paths. He was informed that one path led to the third trial, while the other two led deep into the forest and eventually into large circles, to which there was no end. Xanthius was told that of the signs at the three paths, two were true and one was false. The signs follow:

A
```
The sign at
path B is true.
```

B
```
Path A is not the
one to follow.
```

C
```
This is the
path to follow.
```

Which path is the one to follow?

(Hints on page 45)
(Solution on page 68)

P3-3 The Third Trial*

Again, Xanthius chose correctly and proceeded farther into the forest before the path branched into three more paths. His information this time was that one path led to the fourth trial. The other two led over large hidden pits that could not be avoided, and from which escape would be impossible. Xanthius was told that one of the signs at the three paths was false, and two were true. They read as follows:

A | Path B is the one to follow.

B | Path C is the one to follow, unless it is path A.

C | Neither A nor B is the correct path.

Which path is the one to follow?

(Hints on page 45)
(Solution on pages 68–69)

P3-4 The Fourth Trial*

Xanthius, having made the correct judgment, followed the path until he came to a deep ravine over which were three bridges. He was told that only one of these could carry him over the ravine. The other two would crumble when he was halfway across, dropping him onto the jagged rocks far below. He was informed that two of the three signs at the three bridges were false, and one was true. The three signs follow:

A | C is not the bridge to cross unless this bridge is not the one to cross.

B	C
The sign at bridge A is false.	Either bridge A or bridge B is the one to cross.

Which is the correct bridge to cross?

(Hints on pages 45)
(Solution on page 69)

P3-5 The Fifth Trial*

A large open savanna greeted Xanthius as he left the forest after selecting the correct bridge. At this point, the path Xanthius was following branched into four paths. He was informed that a pride of fierce lions lived and hunted in the immediate area. They napped in the afternoon, and the only chance was to proceed very quietly, so as not to waken them. One of the four paths would provide that opportunity. The other three were liberally strewn with twigs and dry leaves, to the extent that exiting the area without alerting the lions would be impossible. Of the four signs at the four paths, he was told that at least two were false. The signs follow:

A	C
Path B is the one to follow or else path C is.	Path D would be an excellent choice only if path C is not.

B	D
Path C would be a wrong choice.	Path A would be an error.

Which path should be followed?

(Hints on page 46)
(Solution on page 70)

23

P3-6 The Sixth Trial**

After successfully selecting the path and exiting the area, Xanthius came upon a wide area with a profusion of many kinds of fragrant flowers, and a branching of his path into five paths. He was informed that one variety of flower that was prevalent in the area caused anyone who chanced to breathe its perfume to fall immediately into a permanent sleep. Only one of the five paths would circumvent these flowers. Xanthius was informed that of the instructional signs at the five paths, at least three were false. The signs follow:

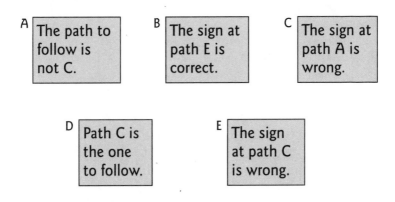

A The path to follow is not C.

B The sign at path E is correct.

C The sign at path A is wrong.

D Path C is the one to follow.

E The sign at path C is wrong.

Only one path is correct. Which one is it?

(Hints on page 46)

(Solution on pages 70–71)

P3-7 The Final Trial**

As a true disciple of Socrates, Xanthius made correct evaluative judgments through the first six trials. He found the seventh trial at the foot of a high mountain. Seven paths led high up on the face of the mountain and disappeared in the clouds. Xanthius was told that one of the paths led to a cave containing the treasure, while the other six paths climbed ever more steeply until the climber could only struggle in place until overcome by exhaustion. Of the seven signs placed at the paths, Xanthius was informed that four were true and three were false. The signs follow:

A | This path or B is the one to follow.

B | The sign at path F is not correct.

C | Path G would be a good choice.

D | This path is the one to take, or else it is E or F.

E | If A is not the correct path, then the right path is C or G.

F | Either C is the right path or else it is B.

G | The sign at path C is wrong.

Xanthius, after lengthy deliberation, selected the correct path and followed it to a cave high on the mountain, where he found the fabulous treasure that he had earned. Which path did he take?

(Hints on page 46)
(Solution on pages 71–72)

—4—

Problems from the Addled Arithmetician

Letters and numbers—to the Addled Arithmetician they are much the same thing. At least it appears so, as he has them reversed.

In this section you will find addition, subtraction, and multiplication problems that he has prepared. Your challenge is to replace the letters with the correct digit. (A zero never appears as the leftmost digit of a number.)

As if mixing digits with letters was not confusing enough, the Addled Arithmetician has forgotten that each letter should represent the same digit wherever it occurs in a puzzle.

In these puzzles, each letter represents the same digit wherever it occurs in a given mathematical problem (above the line). Wherever a letter appears in the answer to the problem (below the line) it represents a digit that is one more than or one less than the digit represented by the same letter above the line. For example, if B equals 4 above the line, all B's below the line will be equal to either 3 or 5.

P4-1 Addition, Six Digits*

Each letter above the line represents a digit that has a difference of one from the digit represented by the same letter below the line.

The digits are 0, 1, 2, 3, 4, and 5.

	A	F	C	E
+	A	D	D	B
	B	F	B	F

What digit or digits are represented by each letter?

(Hints on page 46)

(Solution on page 73)

P4-2 Subtraction, Six Digits*

Each letter above the line represents a digit that has a difference of one from the digit represented by the same letter below the line.

The digits are 0, 1, 2, 3, 4, and 5.

	F	B	A	C	B
−	D	A	F	E	B
		C	F	D	E

What digit or digits are represented by each letter?

(Hints on page 46)

(Solution on page 74)

P4-3 Addition, Seven Digits*

Each letter above the line in this puzzle represents a digit that has a difference of one from the digit represented by the same letter below the line.

The digits are 0, 1, 2, 3, 4, 5, and 6.

	D	G	A	E	C
+	E	F	B	A	C
C	F	G	D	G	F

What digit or digits does each letter represent?

(Hints on page 46)
(Solution on page 75)

P4-4 Addition, Seven Digits Again*

Each letter above the line represents a digit that has a difference of one from the digit represented by the same letter below the line.

The digits are: 0, 1, 2, 3, 4, 8, and 9.

	E	D	B	D	D
	E	D	B	D	D
+	E	D	B	D	D
C	F	A	B	D	E

What digit or digits are represented by each letter?

(Hints on page 47)
(Solution on page 76)

P4-5 Multiplication, Six Digits**

Each letter in the multiplication problem (above the top line) represents a digit that has a difference of one from the digit represented by the same letter in the answer to the problem (below the top line).

The digits are 0, 1, 2, 3, 4, and 5.

```
                C    A    E
          ×     E    C    E
                E    C    A
           D    F    B
      E    C    A
      E    B    B    B    A
```

What digit or digits are represented by each letter?

(Hints on page 47)
(Solution on pages 77–78)

P4-6 Subtraction, Seven Digits**

Each letter above the line represents a digit that has a difference of one from the digit represented by the same letter below the line.

The digits are 0, 1, 2, 3, 4, 5, and 6.

```
    B    D    C    A    B    F    B
 -  E    E    B    G    E    A    E
         G    E    E    F    C    F
```

What digit or digits does each letter represent?

(Hints on page 47)
(Solution on pages 78–79)

P4-7 Addition, Seven Digits Once Again**

Each letter above the line represents a digit that has a difference of one from the digit represented by the same letter below the line.

The digits are 0, 1, 2, 3, 4, 5, and 6.

				F	C	C
			F	A	C	C
		B	A	E	C	A
+	A	D	C	F	A	A
	A	C	B	A	C	A

What digit or digits are represented by each letter?

(Hints on page 47)

(Solution on pages 79–80)

P4-8 Multiplication, Seven Digits**

Each letter in the problem (above the top line) represents a digit that has a difference of one from the digit represented by the same letter in the answer (below the top line).

The digits are 0, 2, 3, 5, 6, 8, and 9.

		D	E	B
×			D	G
		E	E	E
	B	F	G	
	A	E	C	E

What digit or digits are represented by each letter?

(Hints on page 47)

(Solution on pages 80–81)

—5—

What's in a Name?

A rose by any other name would smell as sweet. In these puzzles, the name's the thing: characters in a play, man's best friends, author's pseudonyms, steeds, or other kinds of names. Your challenge is to correctly connect the names of individuals with other names.

P5-1 Four Horses*

Alice, Danielle, Harriet, and Mary each own a horse and enjoy riding together. One day they decided to trade horses for the afternoon. Each woman rode a horse owned by one of the others, and no two women traded horses. From the statements below, what is the name of each friend's horse (one is Champ), and what is the name of the horse each rode?

1. Harriet rode the horse owned by Danielle.
2. Mary's horse was ridden by the owner of the horse named Charger.
3. The horse named El Cid was ridden by the owner of the horse ridden by Alice.
4. The horse named Charger was ridden by the owner of the horse ridden by Harriet.
5. The horse named Silver was ridden by the owner of the horse named El Cid.

(Hints on page 48)
(Solution on pages 81–82)

P5-2 Five Thespians*

Five local actors presented a murder mystery play in the Midville Theater. The five actors were Raymond, Rodney, Roland, Ronald, and Rupert. The five characters in the play were, interestingly enough, all namesakes of the actors, although no actor performed the role of his namesake. The parts in the play were magistrate, murderer, sheriff, victim, and witness. Based on the following, what was each actor's part and what was the name of the character he played?

1. The character played by Raymond was the namesake of the actor who played the murderer.
2. The namesake of the actor who played the magistrate was the character that was the murderer.
3. The character that was the sheriff was played by the actor whose namesake was the character played by Rupert.
4. The character played by Roland was the namesake of the actor who played the witness.
5. Roland did not play the victim, murderer, or sheriff.
6. The character played by Ronald was the namesake of the actor who played the magistrate.
7. The character that was the victim was played by the actor whose namesake was the character played by Rodney.
8. The namesake of the actor who played the murderer was the character that was the victim.

(Hints on page 48)
(Solution on pages 82–83)

P5-3 Five Authors*

Authors James Blackledge, Sarah Hastings, John Montague, Milton Quincy, and Florence Williams met at a convention.

In a casual conversation, they were surprised to discover that each writes using a pseudonym that is the surname of one of the others. Further, no two writers use the same pseudonym. Based on the following statements, what pseudonym does each use and what is the category of book that each authors?

1. The one who writes historical novels, who is not Sarah, uses as a pseudonym the surname of the author of mystery novels.
2. John's surname is used as the pseudonym of the author of mystery novels.
3. The one who writes mystery novels had one of his books on a bestseller list.
4. Milton, who writes general fiction, uses the surname of the author of biographies as his pseudonym.
5. Blackledge is the pseudonym of the writer whose surname is used as the pseudonym of the author of travel books.
6. The surname of the author of historical novels is used as the pseudonym of the author of travel books, who considers that the research involved is his favorite recreation.

(Hints on page 48)
(Solution on pages 83–84)

P5-4 St. Bernards and Dalmations**

Four friends, Sam, Sidney, Simon, and Smitty, enjoy dogs, and each has a St. Bernard and a Dalmatian. Each friend has named his two dogs after two of the other three friends. There are no duplicate names among the four St. Bernards and no duplicate names among the four Dalmatians.

Based on the following statements, what is the name of each owner's dog?

1. Simon's St. Bernard is the namesake of the owner of the Dalmatian named Sidney.
2. Smitty's Dalmatian is the namesake of the owner of which Sam's St. Bernard is the namesake.
3. The Dalmatian named Sam is owned by the owner of which Smitty's St. Bernard is the namesake.
4. Sam's Dalmatian is the namesake of the owner of the St. Bernard named Simon.
5. Sidney's Dalmatian is the namesake of the owner of the St. Bernard named Smitty.

(Hints on page 49)
(Solution on pages 84–85)

P5-5 Islanders' Boats**

Of four friends, O'Boyle, O'Brien, O'Bradovich, and O'Byrne, each has one daughter, spends considerable time on the water, and has both a sailboat and a fishing boat. Each friend has named his two boats after two different daughters of the other three friends. There are no duplicate names among the four sailboats and no duplicate names among the four fishing boats. Based on the following statements, who is the daughter of each of the four friends (one daughter is named Odette), and what are the names of each owner's boats?

1. O'Byrne's fishing boat is named after the owner's daughter after which O'Boyle's sailboat is named.
2. Neither Olivia O'Boyle nor Ophelia O'Byrne enjoys boating.
3. O'Byrne's sailboat is named for the daughter of the owner of the fishing boat named Olivia.
4. O'Brien's fishing boat, which is not named Olga, is named after the daughter of the owner of the sailboat named Ophelia.

5. O'Bradovich's fishing boat is not named Ophelia, nor is his sailboat named Olivia.

(Hints on page 49)
(Solution on pages 85–86)

P5-6 Writers of Classic Books***

Six couples, the Brontës, the Conrads, the Dickenses, the Forsters, the Kafkas, and the Tolstoys, belong to a classics book club. Recently, they exchanged gifts of books. Each couple gave a book to one of the other couples. Each couple is the namesake of the author of one of the books given; no two couples gave a book by the same author; and no couple gave or received a book by an author of which they were the namesakes. The following statements apply:

1. The Conrads did not give or receive a book by Brontë, Forster, or Tolstoy.
2. The namesakes of the author of the book given by the Dickenses gave a book by Dickens to the Tolstoys.
3. The book by Forster was received by the namesakes of the author of the book that was given to the couple who gave the book by Dickens to the namesakes of the author of the book received by the Forsters.
4. The Brontës received a book by Conrad from the name-sakes of the author of the book given by the Conrads.
5. The namesakes of the author of the book received by the Dickenses gave a book by Forster to the namesakes of the author of the book given by the namesakes of the author of the book given by the Kafkas.

Which couples gave books by which authors, and who received them?

(Hints on page 49)
(Solution on page 87–88)

—6—

Land, Valley, and Hill Liars

In the Land of Liars, there are those who speak the truth only in the morning and lie in the afternoon. They are called Amtrus. There are also those who speak the truth only in the afternoon and lie in the morning. They are known as Pemtrus.

If it were only that simple. You will also find (puzzles 6-6 through 6-9) some do not fit the traditional Land of Liars veracity patterns. More on them later.

P6-1 Two Inhabitants*

Two inhabitants make the statements below. One is an Amtru and one is a Pemtru.

A. It is afternoon.
B. I am a Pemtru.

Is it morning or afternoon, which is the Amtru, and which is the Pemtru?

(Hints on page 50)
(Solution on page 88)

P6-2 Is A's Statement True?*

Of the three who make the following statements, two are Pemtrus and one is an Amtru.

A. B is a Pemtru.
B. A's statement is true.
C. A's statement is false.

Is it morning or afternoon, and to which group does each inhabitant belong?

(*Hints on page 50*)
(*Solution on page 89*)

P6-3 Three Inhabitants*

Two Pemtrus and an Amtru make the statements below:

A. B is a Pemtru.
B. C is a Pemtru.
C. A is the Amtru.

Is it morning or afternoon, which is the Amtru, and which are the Pemtrus?

(*Hints on page 50*)
(*Solution on pages 89–90*)

P6-4 Four Inhabitants**

Four inhabitants make the following statements. They are two Amtrus and two Pemtrus.

A. B is an Amtru.
B. C is a Pemtru.
C. A and D are from different groups.
D. A and B are from the same group.

Is it morning or afternoon, and to which group does each of the four inhabitants belong?

(*Hints on page 51*)
(*Solution on page 90*)

P6-5 Five Inhabitants***

Five inhabitants are asked to which group each belongs. They are three Amtrus and two Pemtrus. They respond:

A. I am a Pemtru or it is morning.
B. I am an Amtru or it is afternoon.
C. D and E belong to the same group.
D. A is an Amtru.
E. B is a Pemtru.

Is it morning or afternoon, which ones are Amtrus, and which ones are Pemtrus?

(Hints on page 51)
(Solution on pages 91–92)

Valley Liars

In the Land of Liars, there is a valley in which the inhabitants have their own lying patterns. The Amtrus speak the truth in the morning and lie in the afternoon, except that in statements in which they directly refer to another individual in the same group by name (letter designation), they lie in the morning and speak the truth in the afternoon. The Pemtrus speak the truth in the afternoon and lie in the morning, except that in statements in which they directly refer to another in the same group by name, they lie in the afternoon and speak the truth in the morning.

P6-6 Four Valley Inhabitants**

Four valley inhabitants, who are represented equally by both groups, are asked to which group each belongs. They make the statements below, although the fourth valley inhabitant, D, chooses to remain silent.

A. D and I belong to the same group.
B. A and I belong to the same group.
C. B is a Pemtru.

Is it morning or afternoon, and which group is represented by each of the four inhabitants?

(Hints on page 51)

(Solution on page 92)

P6-7 Three Valley Inhabitants***

Asked their groups, three valley inhabitants respond as follows:

A. C and I are both Pemtrus.
B. C and I are not both Amtrus.
C. If you were to ask A about this guy [pointing to B] and A used this guy's name, A would say that this guy is an Amtru.

Is it morning or afternoon, and which group is represented by each of the three speakers?

(Hints on page 51)

(Solution on page 93)

Liars on the Hill

On a small isolated hill in the Land of Liars live a few who are obstinate and who pride themselves on being different. They are neither Amtrus nor Pemtrus. In making statements when in the company of other inhabitants of the Land of Liars, a hill inhabitant will speak the truth only if none of the others speak the truth, and will lie if any of the others speak the truth.

P6-8 Does C Live on the Hill?**

It is afternoon. Of the four speakers, exactly one is a hill inhabitant. C claims he is the one. Their statements follow:

A. B is an Amtru.
B. C is a Pemtru.
C. I live on the hill.
D. A is a Pemtru.

Which speaker is the hill inhabitant and what are the other three?

(Hints on page 51)
(Solution on page 94)

P6-9 One from the Hill***

Four from the Land of Liars, including exactly one hill inhabitant, make the following statements:

A. Either D is an Amtru or he lives on the hill.
B. C is either an Amtru or a Pemtru.
C. I live on the hill or B lives on the hill.
D. C's statement is true or C is a Pemtru.

Is it morning or afternoon, which one is the hill inhabitant, and what are the other three speakers?

(Hints on page 51)
(Solution on page 95)

HINTS

H1   Prince Tal's Adventures

H1-1   Educational Accomplishments Construct a diagram such as the following:

	chivalry	fencing	riding
excelled			
did well			

Indicate + or – on it as you draw your conclusions. What can you conclude from statements 1 and 3?

H1-2   Battles with Dragons A diagram like this is helpful:

	Biter	Blackheart	Dante	Flame Thrower	Old Smoky
Sir Aard					
Sir Bolbo					
Sir Delfo					

Consider statements 2 and 4. What do they tell you about which nobleman encountered Flame Thrower?

H1-3   Who Tilted with Whom? Prepare a diagram such as the one below:

	Sir Aard	Sir Bolbo	Sir Delfo	Sir Gath	Sir Keln	Prince Tal
Sir Aard						
Sir Bolbo						
Sir Delfo						
Sir Gath						
Sir Keln						
Prince Tal						

Consider statements 1, 3, and 4. What do they tell you about Sir Aard and Sir Keln?

H1-4 Encounter with the Fearsome Beast Use a diagram:

	climbed a tree	prostrate on the ground	was not thrown
Sir Aard			
Sir Bolbo			
Sir Delfo			
Prince Tal			

Consider statement 3. If the assumption is valid, what happened to Sir Delfo?

H1-5 Strange Creatures Construct a diagram like this:

	basilisk	bonnacon	leucrota	monoceros	satyr
Sir Aard					
Sir Bolbo					
Sir Delfo					
Sir Keln					
Prince Tal					

Start with statement 7. Compare it to 1 and 6.

H1-6 Prince Tal and the Enchantress Prepare a diagram such as the following:

	door open	stormed castle	ransom paid	broke door
one day				
three days				
one week				
two weeks				

Start by comparing statements 1 and 2. Attempt to correlate potential lengths of time of imprisonment with different ways of release as you review all seven statements in this puzzle.

H1-7 To the Rescue Construct a diagram like this one:

	Marie	Marion	Mary	Matilda	Morgana	Muriel
Sir Aard						
Sir Bolbo						
Sir Delfo						
Sir Keln						
Prince Tal						

This puzzle requires grouping more than two statements to determine whether or not an assumption is valid. Start with statement 1. Follow a pattern by relating to other statements.

H1-8 Prince Tal's Encounters with Four Dragons Prepare a diagram such as the following:

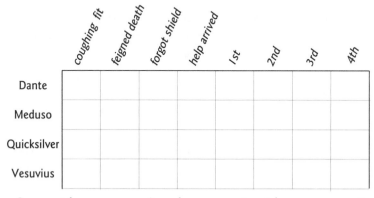

Start with statement 8 and compare it with statements 5, 6, and 7. What can you conclude at this point?

H2 Dragons of Lidd and Wonk

H2-1 One Dragon Is the statement true or false? In either case, what type is the dragon?

For puzzles **2-2** to **2-9** construct diagrams on this order (two, three, or four columns as needed):

	A	B	C
Color			
Type			

Indicate red, gray, or blue, and rational or predator in the coordinates provided.

H2-2 Two Dragons Could A be from Wonk?

H2-3 Three Dragons Could A's second statement be false?

H2-4 Two Are from Wonk Consider that two of the three dragons are blue. Could A's and B's first statements both be false?

H2-5 One Dragon from Wonk Consider that one dragon is blue. Consider A's first and second statements and C's first statement. What can you conclude?

H2-6 At Least One from Wonk Consider that at least one dragon is blue. What can be concluded from A's first statement?

H2-7 Three Dragons Again If A's first statement is true, what can be concluded about A? What about if A's first statement is false?

H2-8 How Many Are Protected? Compare A's second statement, B's first statement, and C's first statement. If A's statement is true, what can you conclude? How about if A's statement if false?

H2-9 Who Speaks for Whom? A's second statement and C's second statement are in agreement. If true, A is a gray rational and C is either a gray rational or a red predator. Is this consistent with their statements regarding B and B's statements?

H3 The Trials of Xanthius
H3-1 The First Trial
Consider that at least one of the signs was false. Since they are in agreement, what can you conclude?

For puzzles **3-2** to **3-7**, prepare a diagram similar to the following. Indicate T or F, considering each path in turn to be the correct one:

	sign A	sign B	sign C
if path A			
if path B			
if path C			

H3-2 The Second Trial Consider that two signs were true and one was false. Could sign C be the path to follow? If not, why not?

H3-3 The Third Trial Consider that one of the three signs was false and two were true. Could path A be the one to follow? If not, why not?

H3-4 The Fourth Trial Consider that, in this trial, two of the three signs were false and one was true. Could bridge B be the one to cross over? If it is not, why not?

H3-5 The Fifth Trial Consider that at least two of the signs were false. Could path D be the one to follow? If not, why not?

H3-6 The Sixth Trial Consider that at least three signs were false. Could path A be the one to follow? If not, why not?

H3-7 The Final Trial Consider that, of the seven signs, four were true and three were false. Could path F be the one to follow? If not, why not?

H4 Problems from the Addled Arithmetician

Note that, for these puzzles, each letter represents the same digit wherever it occurs in a given mathematical problem (above the line). Wherever a letter appears in the answer to the problem (below the line), it represents a number that has a difference of one from the digit represented by the same letter above the line. If a given letter represents 4 above the line, it must represent 3 or 5 below the line.

Make a list of the letters then match the digits above and below the line as they become known to you by carefully considering known mathematical facts.

H4-1 Addition, Six Digits The digits are 0, 1, 2, 3, 4 and 5. Since the largest available digit is 5, what are the possible digits for A? How about B, left-hand column?

H4-2 Subtraction, Six Digits The digits are 0, 1, 2, 3, 4, and 5. What is the only possibility for E below the line?

H4-3 Addition, Seven Digits The digits are 0, 1, 2, 3, 4, 5, and 6. What is the only possibility for C below the line? What are the possibilities for C above the line? How about F below the line?

H4-4 Addition, Seven Digits Again The digits are 0, 1, 2, 3, 4, 8, and 9. There are only two possibilities for D above the line (second column from the right). In examining this, consider the possibilities for D below the line.

H4-5 Multiplication, Six Digits The digits are 0, 1, 2, 3, 4, and 5. What are the possibilities for E above the line? In considering this, think about E times a three-digit number.

H4-6 Subtraction, Seven Digits The digits are 0, 1, 2, 3, 4, 5, and 6. In the left end column in the problem, what can you say about the relationship between B and E? Consider the same letters in the right end column.

H4-7 Addition, Seven Digits Once Again The digits are 0, 1, 2, 3, 4, 5, and 6. Consider that in the left end column A is found both above and below the line. What does that tell you about the addition of B and D in the adjacent column? What are the two possibilities for C below the line?

H4-8 Multiplication, Seven Digits The digits are 0, 2, 3, 5, 6, 8, and 9. There is no digit 1 in the puzzle. Therefore, what can you conclude about 0 above and below the line?

H5 What's in a Name?

Characters and their namesakes can create confusion and require careful attention to each statement in order to reach correct solutions.

  These puzzles are different from the others in the book in that correct interpretation of the statements themselves can be challenging. Careful attention must be paid to all of the possibilities within each statement. Set out the pertinent data, including possibilities, in tabular form. Incorrect considerations can then be eliminated when they are revealed as such.

H5-1   Four Horses Set up a diagram like this. As you form conclusions, insert the names of the horses.

	Alice	Danielle	Harriet	Mary
horse owned				
horse rode				

Consider statements 2, 4, and 1. Who owned Charger?

5-2   Five Thespians Construct a diagram. Indicate plus or minus as you form each conclusion. Insert the names of the characters in the right-hand column.

	magistrate	murderer	sheriff	victim	witness	character
Raymond						
Rodney						
Roland						
Ronald						
Rupert						

Consider statements 4 and 5. What role did Roland play?

H5-3   Five Authors A diagram like this one will be helpful. As you draw conclusions, indicate pluses and minuses. As you determine each author's pseudonym, indicate it in the right-hand column.

	biography	general	historical	mysteries	travel	pseudonym
James						
Sarah						
John						
Milton						
Florence						

From statements 2, 3, and 4, who writes mystery novels?

H5-4 St. Bernards and Dalmatians A diagram like this will be helpful. Indicate each dog's name as you determine it.

	Sam	Sidney	Simon	Smitty
St. Bernard				
Dalmatian				

From statement 1, what are the possible names for Simon's St. Bernard?

H5-5 Islanders' Boats A diagram such as this will be helpful. As you determine the correct daughters' names, insert them in their proper places.

	O'Boyle	O'Bradovich	O'Brien	O'Byrne
daughter				
sailboat				
fishing boat				

From 2, 4, and 5, whose fishing boat is named Ophelia?

H5-6 Writers of Classic Books On a diagram such as this, indicate G (given) or R (received) in the proper places.

	Brontë	Conrad	Dickens	Forster	Kafka	Tolstoy
Brontës						
Conrads						
Dickenses						
Forsters						
Kafkas						
Tolstoys						

From statement 1, what are the possible writers' books given and received by the Conrads?

H6 Land, Valley, and Hill Liars

Prepare a diagram for each puzzle, depicting Amtru and Pemtru on one axis and the letter representing each speaker on the other axis. Assume either morning or afternoon and test the consistency of the speakers' statements against your assumption.

The first 5 puzzles represent traditional Land of Liars standards of veracity. The Amtrus speak the truth in the morning and lie in the afternoon. The Pemtrus speak the truth in the afternoon and lie in the morning.

Puzzles **6-6** and **6-7** represent inhabitants of a valley whose patterns of veracity are traditional except that in statements in which Amtrus refer directly to other Amtrus, they speak the truth in the afternoon and lie in the morning. In statements in which Pemtrus refer directly to other Pemtrus, they speak the truth in the morning and lie in the afternoon.

Puzzles **6-8** and **6-9** represent inhabitants of an isolated hill whose patterns are different. When in the company of other inhabitants of the Land of Liars, they will speak the truth only if none of the others speak the truth; they will lie if any of the others speak the truth.

H6-1 Two Inhabitants One speaker is an Amtru, the other is a Pemtru. What can you say about A's statement?

H6-2 Is A's Statement True? Two of the speakers are Pemtrus, and one is an Amtru. A states that B is a Pemtru. What are the possibilities for A?

H6-3 Three Inhabitants Two of these speakers are Pemtrus, and one is an Amtru. C claims that A is the Amtru. Test C's statement, considering both morning and afternoon.

H6-4 Four Inhabitants Two speakers are Amtrus, and two are Pemtrus. Test A's statement against the other speakers, considering both morning and afternoon.

H6-5 Five Inhabitants Three of the speakers are Amtrus, and two are Pemtrus. Consider that if either part of A's or B's statement is true, the statement is true. D says that A is an Amtru. Consider the possibilities for A.

H6-6 Four Valley Inhabitants Two of the speakers are Amtrus, and two are Pemtrus. Assume it is afternoon. Consider the possibilities for C.

H6-7 Three Valley Inhabitants The number in each group is unknown. Start by analyzing A's statement. If it is afternoon, what can you conclude from B's and C's statements?

H6-8 Does C Live on the Hill? One of the speakers is a hill inhabitant. Consider C's statement. Could it be true?

H6-9 One from the Hill One of the speakers is a hill inhabitant. Assume C is the hill inhabitant. Test this against the statements by the other speakers.

SOLUTIONS

S1-1 Educational Accomplishments

CONSIDERATIONS
From statement 1, if Prince Tal excelled in chivalry, his second subject was horsemanship. However, from statement 3, if he did especially well in horsemanship, he excelled in fencing. From these two statements we can conclude that the hypothesis in statement 1 is invalid. Prince Tal did not excel in chivalry.

From statements 4 and 5, if Prince Tal excelled in fencing, his second subject was chivalry. However, if his second subject was chivalry, he excelled in horsemanship. Therefore, he did not excel in fencing. Therefore, statement 2 is valid.

	chivalry	fencing	riding
excelled	–	–	+
did well	–	+	–

SUMMARY SOLUTION Prince Tal excelled in horsemanship and did especially well in fencing.

S1-2 Battles with Dragons

CONSIDERATIONS
From statement 2, Sir Aard encountered neither Flame Thrower nor Old Smoky. From statement 4, Sir Bolbo encountered neither Flame Thrower nor Black Heart. Therefore, Sir Delfo encountered Flame Thrower.

From statement 6, Sir Delfo did not encounter Biter or Old Smoky. Therefore, Sir Bolbo must have encountered Old Smoky.

From statements 3 and 1, since we know that Sir Delfo

encountered Flame Thrower, Sir Aard did not encounter Dante and Sir Delfo did not encounter Black Heart. From statement 5, since Sir Delfo encountered Flame Thrower, he did not encounter Dante. Therefore, Sir Bolbo encountered Dante and Sir Aard encountered Biter and Black Heart.

	Biter	Blackheart	Dante	Flame Thrower	Old Smoky
Sir Aard	+	+	–	–	–
Sir Bolbo	–	–	+	–	+
Sir Delfo	–	–	–	+	–

SUMMARY SOLUTION

Sir Aard encountered Biter and Black Heart.
Sir Bolbo encountered Dante and Old Smoky.
Sir Delfo encountered Flame Thrower.

S1-3 Who Tilted with Whom?

CONSIDERATIONS

According to statement 1, if either Prince Tal or Sir Aard tilted with Sir Keln, Sir Bolbo tilted with Sir Gath. However, from statements 4 and 3, if Sir Gath and Sir Bolbo tilted, so did Sir Delfo and Prince Tal, and then Sir Keln tilted with Sir Gath. Therefore, Sir Keln did not tilt with Prince Tal or Sir Aard.

From statement 6, if Sir Keln tilted with Sir Gath, Prince Tal tilted with Sir Aard. However, from statement 5, if Prince Tal and Sir Aard tilted, so did Sir Bolbo and Sir Gath. Therefore, Sir Keln did not tilt with Sir Gath.

From statement 3, since Sir Keln did not tilt with Sir Gath, Prince Tal did not tilt with Sir Delfo, and from statement 7, since Sir Keln did not tilt with Sir Aard, Prince Tal did not tilt with Sir Bolbo. Therefore, Prince Tal must have tilted with either Sir Aard or Sir Gath. From statements 5 and 4, if Prince Tal tilted with Sir Aard, then Sir Bolbo and Sir Gath tilted; this, however, means that Sir Delfo and Prince Tal tilted—an impossibility. Therefore, Prince Tal tilted with Sir Gath. From statement 2, Sir Keln tilted with Sir Delfo.

The remaining knights, Sir Bolbo and Sir Aard, tilted with each other.

	Sir Aard	Sir Bolbo	Sir Delfo	Sir Gath	Sir Keln	Prince Tal
Sir Aard	–	+	–	–	–	–
Sir Bolbo	+	–	–	–	–	–
Sir Delfo	–	–	–	–	+	–
Sir Gath	–	–	–	–	–	+
Sir Keln	–	–	+	–	–	–
Prince Tal	–	–	–	+	–	–

SUMMARY SOLUTION
Sir Bolbo tilted with Sir Aard.
Sir Keln tilted with Sir Delfo.
Prince Tal tilted with Sir Gath.

S1-4 Encounter with the Fearsome Beast

CONSIDERATIONS
According to statement 3, if Sir Aard was prostrate on the ground, Prince Tal and Sir Bolbo were not thrown. If this was the case, Sir Delfo was the one who climbed a tree. However, from statement 2, if Sir Delfo climbed a tree, Sir Aard was not thrown. Therefore, Sir Aard was not the one who was prostrate on the ground.

According to statement 1, if Sir Bolbo climbed a tree, Prince Tal and Sir Delfo were not thrown. If so, Sir Aard was the one who was prostrate on the ground. However, since we know that Sir Aard was not the one who was prostrate on the ground, Sir Bolbo was not the one who climbed a tree.

According to statement 2, if Sir Delfo climbed a tree, Sir Aard and Prince Tal were not thrown. If so, Sir Bolbo was the one who was prostrate on the ground. However, from statement 6, if Sir Bolbo was prostrate on the ground, Sir Delfo was not thrown. Therefore, Sir Delfo did not climb a tree.

According to statement 5, if Prince Tal did not climb a tree, either Sir Bolbo or Sir Delfo climbed a tree. Since we know that neither Sir Bolbo nor Sir Delfo climbed a tree, Prince Tal was the one who climbed a tree. Therefore, Sir Aard must have been one of the two adventurers who were not thrown.

Our conclusions so far are:

	climbed a tree	prostrate on the ground	was not thrown
Sir Aard	–	–	+
Sir Bolbo	–		
Sir Delfo	–		
Prince Tal	+	–	–

According to statement 4, if Sir Aard was not thrown, which we know to be the case, Sir Bolbo was not thrown and Sir Delfo was prostrate on the ground.

SUMMARY SOLUTION

Sir Aard was not thrown.
Sir Bolbo was not thrown.
Sir Delfo was prostrate on the ground.
Prince Tal climbed a tree.

S1-5 Strange Creatures

CONSIDERATIONS

From statement 7, since Sir Delfo saw either a basilisk or a monoceros, Sir Delfo did not see a bonnacon, a satyr, or a leucrota. Therefore, from statement 1, Sir Bolbo did not see a monoceros, and from statement 6, Prince Tal did not see a monoceros. From statement 8, Sir Bolbo did not see a leucrota. From statement 4, since Sir Delfo saw either a basilisk or a monoceros, neither Sir Bolbo nor Sir Aard saw a basilisk.

From statement 2, since we know that Prince Tal did not see a monoceros, Sir Bolbo did not see a bonnacon. Therefore, Sir Bolbo saw a satyr.

Conclusions so far are:

	basilisk	bonnacon	leucrota	monoceros	satyr
Sir Aard	–				–
Sir Bolbo	–	–	–	–	+
Sir Delfo		–	–		–
Sir Keln					–
Prince Tal				–	–

From statement 3, since Sir Aard did not see a satyr, Sir Keln was the one to see a leucrota. From statement 5, since Sir Aard did not see a basilisk, Prince Tal did not see a bonnacon. Therefore, Sir Aard is the one who saw a bonnacon, and Prince Tal saw a basilisk. Therefore, Sir Delfo saw a monoceros.

SUMMARY SOLUTION

Sir Aard saw a bonnacon.
Sir Bolbo saw a satyr.
Sir Delfo saw a monoceros.
Sir Keln saw a leucrota.
Prince Tal saw a basilisk.

S1-6 Prince Tal and the Enchantress

CONSIDERATIONS

From statement 5, if the noblemen stormed the castle, Prince Tal was imprisoned for three days. But this contradicts statement 6, so the noblemen did not storm the castle. If he broke the door, from statement 4, Prince Tal was imprisoned for one week or two weeks. But from statement 6, if his imprisonment was for one week, he did not break the door, so if he broke the door, his imprisonment was for two weeks. This contradicts statement 7, though, so he did not break the door.

If the ransom was paid, then Prince Tal was imprisoned for one week or two weeks, according to statement 4. However, statement 3 says that it's impossible for an imprisonment of two weeks and a ransom payment, so if the ransom was paid, Prince Tal was imprisoned for one week. This contradicts statement 2, though, so the ransom was not paid.

Therefore, the dungeon keeper left the door open. From statement 1, Prince Tal was imprisoned for one day or three days. But, from statement 2, it couldn't have been for one day, so it must have been for three days.

SUMMARY SOLUTION Prince Tal was imprisoned for three days and the dungeon keeper left the door open.

S1-7 To the Rescue

CONSIDERATIONS

From statement 1, if Sir Keln rescued Maid Marion or Maid Mary, Sir Aard rescued Maid Muriel or Maid Marie. Following through statements 3, 5, and 7, if Sir Aard rescued Maid Muriel or Maid Marie, then Prince Tal rescued Maid Mary or Maid Morgana, Sir Bolbo rescued Maid

Matilda or Maid Marion, and Sir Delfo rescued both Maid Muriel and Maid Marie, which is a contradiction. Therefore, Sir Keln did not rescue Maid Marion or Maid Mary.

From statement 6, since we know that Sir Keln did not rescue Maid Marion or Maid Mary, Sir Aard rescued either Maid Marion or Maid Muriel. From statements 3, 5, and 7, Sir Aard did not rescue Maid Muriel or Maid Marie. Therefore, he rescued Maid Marion. From statement 8, since Sir Aard did not rescue Maid Marie, but did rescue Maid Marion, Prince Tal rescued both Maid Matilda and Maid Muriel.

Our conclusions so far are as follows:

	Marie	Marion	Mary	Matilda	Morgana	Muriel
Sir Aard	−	+	−	−	−	−
Sir Bolbo		−		−		−
Sir Delfo		−		−		−
Sir Keln		−	−	−		−
Prince Tal	−	−	−	+	−	+

From statement 2, since Prince Tal rescued Maid Matilda, Sir Bolbo rescued Maid Mary. From statement 4, since Sir Bolbo rescued Maid Mary, Sir Keln rescued Maid Morgana. The remaining maiden, Maid Marie, was rescued by Sir Delfo.

SUMMARY SOLUTION

Sir Aard	Maid Marion
Sir Bolbo	Maid Mary
Sir Delfo	Maid Marie
Sir Keln	Maid Morgana
Prince Tal	Maid Matilda and Maid Muriel

CONSIDERATIONS

From statement 8, Prince Tal must not have forgotten his shield during the first and third encounters, since from statements 5, 6, and 7, it is apparent that he did not feign death during his second encounter. Therefore, the encounter in which Prince Tal forgot his shield and left without fighting must have been the second or fourth one. From statements 5 and 7, if the second encounter was with Dante, Quicksilver, or Vesuvius, Prince Tal did not forget his shield at that time. Further, if the second encounter was with Meduso, it was not the time that Prince Tal left without fighting, since we know that Prince Tal fought Meduso using his peripheral vision. Therefore, Prince Tal forgot his shield at the fourth encounter, and that encounter was not with Meduso.

From statements 1 and 4, Vesuvius was not the first or fourth dragon confronted, since Prince Tal's fellow noblemen did not arrive to save him during the fourth encounter, and if they arrived to save him during the first encounter, it was with Quicksilver. From statement 3, since Prince Tal did not feign death during the fourth encounter, it was not with Dante. Therefore, the fourth encounter was with Quicksilver.

From statement 2, since the fourth encounter was not with Meduso, the first encounter was not with Dante. Therefore, the first encounter was with Meduso.

From statement 6, since the encounter with Meduso was the first one, Prince Tal did not feign death in his confrontation with this dragon. From statement 4, Prince Tal's fellow noblemen did not arrive to save him during the encounter with Meduso. Therefore, the outcome of the encounter with Meduso was that the dragon suffered a coughing fit.

Conclusions so far are:

	coughing fit	feigned death	forgot shield	help arrived	1st	2nd	3rd	4th
Dante	−		−		−			−
Meduso	+	−	−	−	+	−	−	−
Quicksilver	−	−	+	−	−	−	−	+
Vesuvius	−		−		−			−

Either the encounter with Vesuvius or the one with Dante resulted in Prince Tal's fellow noblemen arriving in time to rescue him. From statement 7, the encounter with Vesuvius was not the second one. Therefore, the second encounter was with Dante, and from statement 5, the outcome was that Prince Tal's fellow noblemen rescued him. Therefore, the third encounter was with Vesuvius and the outcome was that Prince Tal feigned death.

SUMMARY SOLUTION
1st encounter	Meduso	coughing fit
2nd encounter	Dante	help arrived
3rd encounter	Vesuvius	feigned death
4th encounter	Quicksilver	forgot shield

S2-1   One Dragon

CONSIDERATIONS
If either part of A's statement is true, the statement is true. A is not blue, as all blue dragons lie. If the statement is true, A is a gray rational; if it is false, A must be a red rational.

SUMMARY SOLUTION   The dragon is a rational.

S2-2 Two Dragons

CONSIDERATIONS

A is not from Wonk, as blue dragons always lie. A's first statement is false, so A is either a red rational or a gray predator. A's second statement is false; at least one of A and B is a rational.

B, who also claims to be from Wonk, has lied. From B's second statement, B is a gray predator. Therefore, A must be a red rational.

	A	B
color	red	gray
type	rational	predator

SUMMARY SOLUTION

A is a red rational.

B is a gray predator.

S2-3 Three Dragons

CONSIDERATIONS

A's second statement is true. If it were false, A would be a red predator, and red predators always tell the truth. A is a gray rational. Therefore, from A's first statement, C is blue.

We know that B's statements are false, since B's first statement claims that A is from Wonk. From B's second statement, since A is a rational, C must be a predator. From C's two statements, which are false, we can conclude that B is a red rational.

	A	B	C
color	gray	red	blue
type	rational	rational	predator

SUMMARY SOLUTION

A is a gray rational.
B is a red rational.
C is a blue predator.

S2-4 Two Are from Wonk

CONSIDERATIONS

Consider that two of the three dragons are blue.

Since blue dragons from Wonk always lie, one of A's and B's first statements, asserting that B and C are from Wonk, must be true and the other false. Thus, one of B and C is not blue. Therefore, A has lied; he must be one of the two from Wonk. Therefore, B has told the truth. B is a gray rational, and A and C are blue predators.

	A	B	C
color	blue	gray	blue
type	predator	rational	predator

SUMMARY SOLUTION

A is a blue predator.
B is a gray rational.
C is a blue predator.

S2-5 One Dragon from Wonk

CONSIDERATIONS

Consider that one dragon is blue.

Assume A is a gray rational as indicated by his second statement. If so, C must be a gray rational, as A's first statement claims. However, from C's first statement, A is not a gray rational. Therefore, A's statements are false, and C's statements are true. C must be a red predator. From C's second statement, B is blue; and, from B's third statement, B is a predator. From B's first and second statements, A is a red rational.

	A	B	C
color	red	blue	red
type	rational	predator	predator

SUMMARY SOLUTION

A is a red rational.
B is a blue predator.
C is a red predator.

S2-6 At Least One from Wonk

CONSIDERATIONS

Consider that at least one dragon is blue.

A must be blue. Only a blue dragon can claim that he is a gray predator or a red rational. B's second statement must be false, since if it were true, C's second statement would be impossible. From B's third statement, B is not gray, and from A's second statement, which is false, B is not red. Therefore, B is blue.

D's third statement correctly asserts that both A and B are blue. Therefore, D is a red predator, as claimed.

C, whose statements are false, is a gray predator. From C's third statement, B is a rational, and from B's first statement, A is a predator.

	A	B	C	D
color	blue	blue	gray	red
type	predator	rational	predator	predator

SUMMARY SOLUTION

A is a blue predator.
B is a blue rational.
C is a gray predator.
D is a red predator.

S2-7 Three Dragons Again

CONSIDERATIONS

If A's first statement is true, A is either a gray rational or a red predator. If his first statement is false, he is either a blue rational or a blue predator. If B's second statement is true, C is blue and from C's first statement, which would be false, A's statements are true. If B's first statement is false, A is red and, again, C's first statement is false. Therefore, in either case, A's statements are true. A is either a gray rational or a red predator.

From A's second statement, C is either gray or red. Therefore, since at least one dragon is blue, it must be B. From B's first statement, which is false, A is a red predator. From A's second statement, C is red, and must be a rational. From C's second statement, B is a rational.

	A	B	C
color	red	blue	red
type	predator	rational	rational

SUMMARY SOLUTION

A is a red predator.
B is a blue rational.
C is a red rational.

S2-8 How Many Are Protected?

CONSIDERATIONS

Assume A's second statement is true. If so, B's statements are false; B is either a red rational or a blue rational. If so, from B's second statement, C could be a red rational or a blue rational. However, C's third statement would be true and first statement would be false, which is not possible. Therefore, A's statements are false.

From A's second statement, at least one of the three must be a predator. From A's first statement, he is either red or blue, and from A's third statement, C is either gray or blue.

Assume that C's statements are true. If so, C is a gray rational; and from C's second statement, A must be a red rational. However, C's first statement indicates that he and A are different types, an inconsistency. Therefore, C's statements are false; A is not red. Therefore, A is blue.

From C's third statement, B is a predator, which is consistent with B's first statement. Therefore, B is a red predator. From B's second statement, C must be a gray predator. From C's first statement, A is a predator.

	A	B	C
color	blue	red	gray
type	predator	predator	predator

SUMMARY SOLUTION

A is a blue predator.
B is a red predator.
C is a gray predator.

S2-9 Who Speaks for Whom?

CONSIDERATIONS

Assume that A's statements are true. If so, from A's second statement, A must be a gray rational. From C's second statement, which agrees with A's second statement, C's statements are also true, and C is either a gray rational or a red predator. If so, from C's first statement and A's third statement, B is a red rational, with all false statements.

However, B's first statement is in agreement with the type that C would claim for A. This statement would not be possible for a red rational. Therefore, A's statements are false.

Therefore, from A's statements, B would claim that C is a rational, A is either red or blue, and B is a predator. C, who asserts that A is gray, is also a liar. From C's first statement, A would claim that B is not red. Therefore, B is red.

B's first statement, that C would claim that A is a rational, is correct. Therefore, B is a red predator, and from B's second statement, C is a red rational. A is a predator, and since we have established that A is a liar and is not gray, A is blue.

	A	B	C
color	blue	red	red
type	predator	predator	rational

SUMMARY SOLUTION

A is a blue predator.
B is a red predator.
C is a red rational.

S3-1 The First Trial

CONSIDERATIONS

Consider that at least one of the signs was false.

The two signs agree. Since at least one was false, they cannot both be true. Therefore, they were both false, and path A would lead to the next trial.

SUMMARY SOLUTION Path A was the one to follow.

S3-2 The Second Trial

CONSIDERATIONS

Consider that two signs were true and one was false.

Assume path A led to the next trial. If so, the signs at all three paths were false. Therefore, path A would be a wrong choice. Assume path C was the one to follow. If so, all three signs were true. Therefore, path C would be a wrong choice. Therefore, path B must be the right choice. The signs at paths A and B were true, and the sign at path C was false.

	sign A	sign B	sign C
if path A	F	F	F
if path B	T	T	F
if path C	T	T	T

SUMMARY SOLUTION Path B is the correct choice.

S3-3 The Third Trial

CONSIDERATIONS

Consider that one of the three signs was false.

Assume A was the path to follow. If so, the sign at path A was false, the sign at path B was true, and the sign at path C was false. Therefore, path A was not the path to follow.

Assume B was the correct path. If so, the sign at path A was true, the sign at path B was false, and the sign at path C was false. Therefore, path B was not the correct path.

C was the correct path. The sign at path A was false, the sign at path B was true, and the sign at path C was true.

	sign A	sign B	sign C
if path A	F	T	F
if path B	T	F	F
if path C	F	T	T

SUMMARY SOLUTION Path C was the one to follow.

S3-4 The Fourth Trial

CONSIDERATIONS
Consider that two of the three signs were false.

Assume bridge A was the one to cross. If so, the sign at bridge A was true, the sign at bridge B was false, and the sign at bridge C was true. Therefore, Bridge A was not the one to cross.

Assume that bridge B was the one to cross. If so, the sign at bridge A was false, the sign at bridge B was true, and the sign at bridge C was true. Therefore, bridge B was not the one to cross.

The bridge to cross was C. The sign at bridge A was true, the sign at bridge B was false, and the sign at bridge C was false.

	sign A	sign B	sign C
if bridge A	T	F	T
if bridge B	F	T	T
if bridge C	T	F	F

SUMMARY SOLUTION Bridge C was the one to cross.

S3-5   The Fifth Trial

Consider that at least two of the signs were false.

Assume that path B led to the next trial. If so, the sign at path A was true, the sign at path B was true, the sign at path C was false, and the sign at path D was true. Therefore, path B was not correct. Assume that path C led to the next trial. If so, the sign at path A was true, the sign at path B was false, the sign at path C was true, and the sign at path D was true. Therefore, path C was not the correct choice. Assume that path D led to the next trial. If so, the sign at path A was false, the sign at path B was true, the sign at path C was true, and the sign at path D was true. Therefore, path D was not correct.

Therefore, path A was the correct choice. The sign at path A was false, the sign at path B was true, the sign at path C was false, and the sign at path D was false.

	sign A	sign B	sign C	sign D
if path A	F	T	F	F
if path B	T	T	F	T
if path C	T	F	T	T
if path D	F	T	T	T

SUMMARY SOLUTION Path A leds to the next trial.

S3-6   The Sixth Trial

CONSIDERATIONS

Consider that at least three of the signs were false.

Assume A was the path to follow. If so, the sign at path A was true, the sign at path B was true, the sign at path C was false, the sign at path D was false, and the sign at path E was true. Therefore, A was not the correct path. Assume

B was the path to follow. If so, the sign at path A was true, the sign at path B was true, the sign at path C was false, the sign at path D was false, and the sign at path E was true. Therefore, B was not the path to follow. Assume that D was the correct path. If so, the sign at path A was true, the sign at path B was true, the sign at path C was false, the sign at path D was false, and the sign at path E was true. Therefore, D was the wrong path. Assume that E was the correct path. If so, the sign at path A was true, the sign at path B was true, the sign at path C was false, the sign at path D was false, and the sign at path E was true. Therefore, path E was the wrong path.

Therefore, path C was the correct path. The sign at path A was false, the sign at path B was false, the sign at path C was true, the sign at path D was true, and the sign at path E was false.

	sign A	sign B	sign C	sign D	sign E
if path A	T	T	F	F	T
if path B	T	T	F	F	T
if path C	F	F	T	T	F
if path D	T	T	F	F	T
if path E	T	T	F	F	T

SUMMARY SOLUTION The correct path was C.

S3-7 The Final Trial

CONSIDERATIONS
Consider that four of the signs were true.

Assume that B was the path to follow. If so, the signs at paths A, F, and G were true, and the signs at B, C, D, and E were false. Therefore, B was not the correct path. Assume that C was the path to follow. If so, the signs at paths E, F, and G were true, and the signs at paths A, B, C, and D were false. Therefore, path C was not the correct path. Assume that D was the correct path. If so, the signs at paths B, D, and G were true, and the signs at A, C, E, and F were false. Therefore, D was wrong. Assume that E was the path to follow. If so, the signs at paths B, D, and G were true and the signs at paths A, C, E, and F were false. Therefore, E was not the path of choice. Assume that F was the correct path. If so, the signs at paths B, D, and G were true, and the signs at paths A, C, E, and F were false. Therefore, F was not the path to follow. Assume that G was the correct path. If so, the signs at paths B, C, and E were true, and the signs at paths A, D, F, and G were false. Therefore, G was not the correct path.

Therefore, A was the path to follow. The signs at paths A, B, E, and G were true, and the signs at paths C, D, and F were false.

	sign A	sign B	sign C	sign D	sign E	sign F	sign G
if path A	T	T	F	F	T	F	T
if path B	T	F	F	F	F	T	T
if path C	F	F	F	F	T	T	T
if path D	F	T	F	T	F	F	T
if path E	F	T	F	T	F	F	T
if path F	F	T	F	T	F	F	T
if path G	F	T	T	F	T	F	F

SUMMARY SOLUTION A was the correct path.

S4-1 Addition, Six Digits

CONSIDERATIONS

Each letter above the line represents a digit that has a difference of one from the digit represented by the same letter below the line.

The digits are 0, 1, 2, 3, 4, and 5.

	(4)	(3)	(2)	(1)
	A	F	C	E
+	A	D	D	B
	B	F	B	F

Since the largest available digit is 5, A must be 1 or 2, and B below the line is 2 or 4. From column 3, since F above the line and F below the line must be one number different, D must be 1. Therefore, A is not 1; A is 2. B below the line is 4, and B above the line is 3 or 5. From column 2, C must be 3, since C plus 1 equals 4. Therefore, B above the line is 5.

Considering the digits left, F above the line must be 4. Therefore, F below the line is 5; and E is 0, the remaining digit.

SUMMARY SOLUTION

A	B	C	D	E	F
2	5	3	1	0	4
	4				5

	2	4	3	0
+	2	1	1	5
	4	5	4	5

CONSIDERATIONS

The digits are 0, 1, 2, 3, 4, and 5.

(5)	(4)	(3)	(2)	(1)
F	B	A	C	B
− D	A	F	E	B
C	F	D	E

From column 1, E below the line equals 0, and E above the line must be 1. From column 5, D above the line is one less than F above the line, since the answer disappears in that column. D above the line must be 4, 3, or 2.

From column 4, since there was a carry from column 5, B must represent a smaller digit than A. Since the largest available digit is 5, the only possibility is A is 5, and B is 0 and C below the line is 5. Therefore, C above the line is 4.

From column 2, D below the line must be 3. From column 5, D above the line cannot be 4, since that digit is taken. Therefore, D above is 2, and F above is 3. From column 3, A minus F equals F. Therefore, since A above is 5, and F above is 3, F below is 2.

SUMMARY SOLUTION

A	B	C	D	E	F
5	0	4	2	1	3
		5	3	0	2

3	0	5	4	0
− 2	5	3	1	0
5	2	3	0

S4-3   Addition, Seven Digits

CONSIDERATIONS

The digits are 0, 1, 2, 3, 4, 5 and 6.

	(5)	(4)	(3)	(2)	(1)
	D	G	A	E	C
+	E	F	B	A	C
C	F	G	D	G	F

C below the line reprints a carry from column 5. C below the line must be 1. Therefore, C above the line is 0 or 2. Therefore, from column 1, F below the line is 0 or 4. If F below is 4, from column 5, then D plus E must equal 14. This is not possible with the available digits. Therefore, F below is 0 and C above is also 0. F above must be 1.

From column 5, since F below is 0, D and E are 6 and 4, or 4 and 6. From column 2, E plus A equals G. Since we know that F below is 0 and C below is 1, there is no combination of digits available in which E could be 6. Therefore, E is 4 and D above is 6. Therefore, D below is 5. The only possible digit available to A is 2, and G below is 6. Therefore, G above is 5. B is 3, the remaining digit.

SUMMARY SOLUTION

A	B	C	D	E	F	G
2	3	0	6	4	1	5
		1	5		0	6

	6	5	2	4	0	
+	4	1	3	2	0	
1	0	6	5	6	0	

S4-4 Addition, Seven Digits Again

CONSIDERATIONS

The digits are 0, 1, 2, 3, 4, 8, and 9.

	(5)	(4)	(3)	(2)	(1)
	E	D	B	D	D
	E	D	B	D	D
+	E	D	B	D	D
C	F	A	B	D	E

D above the line, column 2, must be 4 or 9. No other available digits above the line will equal D below the line given a carry from column 1. However, if D above the line were 9, the carry from column 1 would be 2, and D below the line, column 2, would be 9, the same as D above the line. Therefore, D above the line is 4 and D below the line is 3. E below the line, column 1, must be 2.

Since A represents 4 plus 4 plus 4 plus a different carry than 1, that carry must be 2, and A equals 4.

B above the line must be 9, and B below the line is 8 (9 plus 9 plus 9 plus a carry of 1 from column 2). Given what's left, E above the line is 3, F is 0 (3 plus 3 plus 3 plus a carry of 1 from column 4), and C is 1.

SUMMARY SOLUTION

A	B	C	D	E	F
	9		4	3	
4	8	1	3	2	0

	3	4	9	4	4
	3	4	9	4	4
+	3	4	9	4	4
1	0	4	8	3	2

S4-5 Multiplication, Six Digits

CONSIDERATIONS

Each letter in the problem (above the line) represents a digit that has a difference of one from the digit represented by the same letter in the answer (below the line).

The digits are 0, 1, 2, 3, 4, and 5.

			C	A	E	(1)
		×	E	C	E	(2)
			E	C	A	(3)
		D	F	B		(4)
	E	C	A			(5)
	E	B	B	B	A	(6)

E above the line can't be 0, since it starts a three-digit number. It can't be 3 or 4, since that would make A below be 9 or 6. It can't be 5, since E below would then be 4, and row 1 times 5 can't start with a 4 since C can't be 0. If E above the line were 1, A below the line would also be 1, making A above the line 0 or 2. If A above the line were 0, C below the line, row 3, would also be 0, making C above the line, row 2, 1, which is already taken. If A above the line were 2, C below the line, row 3, would also be 2, making C above the line 3. This would not fit, since F would be 6. Therefore, E above is 2. Therefore, A below the line, is 4.

E, row 2, times C, row 1, equals E, row 3. Therefore, there must be a carry from E times A (since E below must be an odd number). Therefore, E below the line must be 3, and A above the line must be 5.

The remaining letter above the line, C, is 1.

SUMMARY SOLUTION

A	B	C	D	E	F
5		1		2	
4	2	0	1	3	5

```
            1    5    2
    ×       2    1    2
            3    0    4
       1    5    2
  3    0    4
  3    2    2    2    4
```

S4-6 Subtraction, Seven Digits

CONSIDERATIONS

The digits are 0, 1, 2, 3, 4, 5, and 6.

(7)	(6)	(5)	(4)	(3)	(2)	(1)
B	D	C	A	B	F	B
− E	E	B	G	E	A	E
	G	E	E	F	C	F

From column 7, B is one more than E, since the column disappears in the answer to the problem. Therefore, from column 1, F below the line equals 1. Therefore, F above the line is 0 or 2. From column 3, it is apparent that no carry to column 2 is required, since the digit in the answer is the same as for column 1. Therefore, F above the line must be 2, and A is 0 or 1. C below the line must be 2, since 1 is taken. Therefore, A is 0. C above the line must be 1 or 3.

From column 6, considering that a carry from column 7 was required, E above the line must be 5, 4, or 3, and D must be 0, 1, or 2. Therefore, since 0 and 2 are taken, D is 1. Therefore, C above the line is 3, and E above the line is 5 or 4.

From column 6, if E above the line is 4, G below the line must be 6, and B must be 5. If so, however, G above the line must also be 5. Therefore, E above the line is 5, B is 6, and G above the line is 4, the remaining digit above the line. Subtracting yields the rest.

A	B	C	D	E	F	G
0	6	3	1	5	2	4
		2		6	1	5

	A	B	C	D	E	F	G
	6	1	3	0	6	2	6
−	5	5	6	4	5	0	5
		5	6	6	1	2	1

S4-7 Addition, Seven Digits Once Again

CONSIDERATIONS

The digits are 0, 1, 2, 3, 4, 5, and 6.

	(6)	(5)	(4)	(3)	(2)	(1)
				F	C	C
			F	A	C	C
		B	A	E	C	A
+	A	D	C	F	A	A
	A	C	B	A	C	A

From column 6, A below the line represents A above the line plus a carry from column 5. Therefore, the sum of B above the line, D, and the carry into column 5 has to be 10 or more. The carry into column 5 can be no more than 1, so the sum of B above and D has to be 9 or more, and C below is either 0, 1, or 2. That means that C above is 0, 1, 2, or 3, but looking at columns 1 and 2, the only one that makes a value of A above that works in both columns is C above, equal to 0. In this case, A above must be 1, and A below is 2. This makes C below equal to 1. Column 4, with a 1 and a 0, doesn't have enough to carry into column 5, so the sum of B above and D is 11; thus one is 5 and one is 6. Looking at column 3, F + 1 + E + F sums to either 2 or 12. The only numbers left for E and F are 2, 3, and 4, and the only combination that works is F = 4 and E = 3. This makes B below in column 4 equal to 6, which means E above is 5 and D is 6.

SUMMARY SOLUTION

A	B	C	D	E	F
1	5	0	6	3	4
2	6	1			

			4	0	0
		4	1	0	0
	5	1	3	0	1
+ 1	6	0	4	1	1
2	1	6	2	1	2

S4-8 Multiplication, Seven Digits

CONSIDERATIONS

The digits are 0, 2, 3, 5, 6, 8, and 9.

	D	E	B	(1)
×		D	G	(2)
	E	E	E	(3)
B	F	G		(4)
A	E	C	E	(5)

There is no digit 1 in the problem. Therefore, 0 must be represented by a letter that is not both above and below the line. The possibilities for 0 are A, C, D, and F. D can be eliminated, since it is located at the left end of lines 1 and 2. A can be eliminated, since it represents a digit one number greater than B below the line, resulting from a carry from E below plus F. Additionally, since there is a carry from E below plus F, F must be greater than 0. Therefore, C is 0.

The multipliers, D and G above, line 2, must be 2 and 3 or 3 and 2, since neither digit creates a carry that results in a fourth digit in rows 3 or 4. D must be 2, since if it were 3, D times D plus a carry from E above times D would create a fourth digit in line 4. Therefore, G above the line is 3, and

G below the line must be 2 since there is no 4 available.

B below the line must be 5 or 8 and A must be 6 or 9. B above the line must be 6 or 9. However, 3 times 9 (B above times G above) would yield 7, a digit not available. Therefore, B above the line is 6, B below the line is 5, and A is 6.

E below the line must be 8 since B above times G above equals 18 (lines 1, 2 and 3). Therefore, E above the line is 9, and F equals 9, since E below plus F plus a carry equals E below (lines 3, 4, and 5).

SUMMARY SOLUTION

A	B	C	D	E	F	G
	6		2	9		3
6	5	0		8	9	2

$$
\begin{array}{ccc}
 & 2 & 9 & 6 \\
\times & & 2 & 3 \\
\hline
 & 8 & 8 & 8 \\
5 & 9 & 2 & \\
\hline
6 & 8 & 0 & 8 \\
\end{array}
$$

S5-1   Four Horses

CONSIDERATIONS

From statement 2, Mary did not own or ride the horse named Charger. From statements 1 and 4, Danielle rode Charger, so neither Danielle nor Harriet owned Charger. Therefore, Charger was owned by Alice.

From statements 3 and 5, since Alice did not ride El Cid or Silver, she rode Champ. Since Champ's owner rode El Cid, and El Cid's owner rode Silver, Danielle owned Silver. Then, from statement 1, Harriet owned El Cid and rode Silver, and Mary owned Champ and rode El Cid.

	Alice	Danielle	Harriet	Mary
horse owned	Charger	Silver	El Cid	Champ
horse rode	Champ	Charger	Silver	El Cid

SUMMARY SOLUTION

	horse owned	horse rode
Alice	Charger	Champ
Danielle	Silver	Charger
Harriet	El Cid	Silver
Mary	Champ	El Cid

S5-2 Five Thespians

CONSIDERATIONS

From statements 4 and 5, Roland did not play the victim, the murderer, the sheriff, or the witness. Therefore, Roland played the magistrate. From statements 6 and 2, we can conclude that Ronald played Roland the murderer. From statements 1 and 8, we can conclude that Raymond's character was Ronald the victim.

Our conclusions at this point are:

	magistrate	murderer	sheriff	victim	witness	character
Raymond	−	−	−	+	−	Ronald
Rodney	−	−		−		
Roland	+	−	−	−	−	
Ronald	−	+	−	−	−	Roland
Rupert	−	−		−		

From statement 7, Rodney played the part of Raymond. Since the two remaining parts are the sheriff and the witness, and since from statement 3, Rupert did not play the sheriff, it is evident that Rodney played the sheriff and

Rupert played the role of Rodney, the witness. The remaining character, Rupert, was the magistrate.

SUMMARY SOLUTION

actor	character	role
Raymond	Ronald	victim
Rodney	Raymond	sheriff
Roland	Rupert	magistrate
Ronald	Roland	murderer
Rupert	Rodney	witness

S5-3 Five Authors

CONSIDERATIONS

From statement 4, Milton writes general fiction. From statements 2 and 3, neither John, Sarah, nor Florence write mystery novels. Therefore, James writes mystery novels, and uses Montague as his pseudonym (statement 2). From statement 6, John must be the author of travel books.

At this point our conclusions are:

	biography	general	historical	mysteries	travel	pseudodym
James	–	–	–	+	–	Montague
Sarah		–		–	–	
John	–	–	–	–	+	
Milton	–	+	–	–	–	
Florence		–		–	–	

From statement 1, Sarah does not write historical novels. Therefore, Florence writes historical novels, and Sarah writes biographies. Also from statement 1, Florence's pseudonym is Blackledge, and from statement 5, John's pseudonym is Williams. Sarah's pseudonym is Quincy, and Milton's pseudonym is Hastings.

James Blackledge	Montague	mystery novels
Sarah Hastings	Quincy	biographies
John Montague	Williams	travel books
Milton Quincy	Hastings	general fiction
Florence Williams	Blackledge	historical novels

S5-4 St. Bernards and Dalmatians

CONSIDERATIONS

From statement 1, we can conclude that Simon's St. Bernard is not named Sidney. Therefore, the name is Sam or Smitty, and Sam or Smitty owns the Dalmatian named Sidney. From statement 2, we can conclude that Smitty's Dalmatian is not named Sam. Therefore, the name is either Sidney or Simon, as is Sam's St. Bernard. From statement 4, we can conclude that Sam's Dalmatian is not named Simon. Therefore, the name is either Sidney or Smitty, and Sidney or Smitty owns the St. Bernard named Simon.

From statement 5, we can conclude that Sidney's Dalmatian is not named Smitty. Therefore, the name is either Sam or Simon, and Sam or Simon owns the St. Bernard named Smitty. From statement 3, we can conclude that the Dalmatian named Sam is not owned by Smitty. Therefore, the owner is Sidney or Simon. Also, Smitty's St. Bernard must be named Sidney or Simon.

From statement 5, we know that Sam or Simon owns the St. Bernard named Smitty. From statement 2, we know that Sam's St. Bernard is named Sidney or Simon. Therefore, Simon must own the St. Bernard named Smitty.

From statement 4, we know that Sam's Dalmatian is named either Sidney or Smitty. Therefore, Sam must own the Dalmatian named Smitty, since the name is not available to any of the other three owners.

From statement 4, we know that Sidney or Smitty owns the St. Bernard named Simon. From statement 2, we know that Sam's St. Bernard is named Sidney or Simon. Therefore, Sam's St. Bernard must be named Sidney. Therefore, Smitty's Dalmatian is named Sidney (from statement 2), and his St. Bernard is named Simon (from statement 3). Our conclusions at this point are:

	Sam	Sidney	Simon	Smitty
St. Bernard	Sidney		Smitty	Simon
Dalmatian	Smitty			Sidney

Therefore, Sidney's St. Bernard is named Sam, Simon's Dalmatian is named Sam, and Sidney's Dalmatian is named Simon.

SUMMARY SOLUTION

owner	St. Bernard	Dalmation
Sam	Sidney	Smitty
Sidney	Sam	Simon
Simon	Smitty	Sam
Smitty	Simon	Sidney

S5-5 Islanders' Boats

CONSIDERATIONS

From statement 2, O'Byrne's daughter is Ophelia. Therefore, his fishing boat is not named Ophelia. From statement 4, O'Brien's fishing boat is not named Ophelia, and from statement 5, O'Bradovich's fishing boat is not named Ophelia. Therefore, that name belongs to O'Boyle's fishing boat. Therefore, O'Boyle's sailboat is not named Ophelia.

From statement 4, O'Brien's sailboat is not named

Ophelia, and, since O'Byrne's sailboat is not named Ophelia (his daughter's name), that name belongs to O'Bradovich's sailboat.

From statement 3, O'Byrne's sailboat is not named Olivia. From statement 2, O'Boyle's daughter is named Olivia. Therefore, O'Brien's sailboat is named Olivia. From statement 4, O'Brien's fishing boat is not named Olga. Therefore, his fishing boat must be named Odette.

Our conclusions, so far, are:

	O'Boyle	O'Bradovich	O'Brien	O'Byrne
daughter	Olivia			Ophelia
sailboat		Ophelia	Olivia	
fishing boat	Ophelia		Odette	

O'Brien's daughter, who is not named Odette, must be named Olga, and O'Bradovich's daughter is Odette.

From statement 1, O'Byrne's fishing boat and O'Boyle's sailboat have the same name. Therefore, the name is not Olivia or Ophelia (their daughters' names). Since O'Brien's fishing boat is named Odette, O'Byrne's fishing boat and O'Boyle's sailboat are both named Olga. Therefore, O'Byrne's sailboat is named Odette, and O'Bradovich's fishing boat is named Olivia.

SUMMARY SOLUTION

owner	daughter	sailboat	fishing boat
O'Boyle	Olivia	Olga	Ophelia
O'Bradovich	Odette	Ophelia	Olivia
O'Brien	Olga	Olivia	Odette
O'Byrne	Ophelia	Odette	Olga

CONSIDERATIONS

From statement 1, the Conrads gave or received a book by Dickens and gave or received a book by Kafka. From statement 2, since the Tolstoys were the ones who received a book by Dickens, it must have been given by the Conrads, who received a book by Kafka. According to statement 4, the Brontës received a book by Conrad from the namesakes of the author of the book given by the Conrads. Therefore, since we know that the Conrads gave a book by Dickens, the Brontës received a book by Conrad from the Dickenses.

Since we know that the Conrads were the couple who received a book by Kafka, from statement 3, a book by Forster was received by the Kafkas. Also, from statement 3, since we know that the Conrads gave a book by Dickens, and that it was given to the Tolstoys, the Forsters received a book by Tolstoy.

Conclusions at this point:

	Brontë	Conrad	Dickens	Forster	Kafka	Tolstoy
Brontës		R				
Conrads			G		R	
Dickenses		G				
Forsters						R
Kafkas				R		
Tolstoys			R			

G = Gave   R = Received

A book by Brontë must have been received by the Dickenses, since this is the remaining possibility.

From statement 5, since we know that the Dickenses

received a book by Brontë, the Brontës gave a book by Forster to the Kafkas. Since (also from statement 5) the namesakes of the book given by the Kafkas (the remaining choices are a book by Brontë or a book by Tolstoy) gave a book by Kafka, the gift given by the Kafkas must have been a book by Tolstoy, and the Tolstoys gave a book by Kafka. Therefore, the Forsters gave a book by Brontë.

SUMMARY SOLUTION

	gave	received
Brontës	Forster	Conrad
Conrads	Dickens	Kafka
Dickenses	Conrad	Brontë
Forsters	Brontë	Tolstoy
Kafkas	Tolstoy	Forster
Tolstoys	Kafka	Dickens

S6-1   Two Inhabitants

CONSIDERATIONS

From A's statement, we know that A is a Pemtru. Only a Pemtru can, truthfully or falsely, state that it is afternoon.

From B's statement, we know that it is afternoon, whether B's statement is truthful or not. In this case, B has made a false statement.

	A	B
Amtru	–	+
Pemtru	+	–

SUMMARY SOLUTION

It is afternoon, A is a Pemtru, and B is an Amtru.

S6-2 Is A's Statement True?

CONSIDERATIONS

Consider that two are Pemtrus.

Assume it is morning. If so, and if A is an Amtru, his statement is true, and B is a Pemtru. However, B's statement would be impossible for a Pemtru in the morning. Therefore, if it is morning, A must be a Pemtru. If so, A's statement is false, and B is an Amtru. However, since A's statement would be false, B's statement would be impossible for an Amtru in the morning.

Therefore, it is afternoon. If A is an Amtru, B is also an Amtru. However, since we know that two are Pemtrus, A is not an Amtru. A is a Pemtru, as is B. C, whose statement is false, is an Amtru.

	A	B	C
Amtru	–	–	+
Pemtru	+	+	–

SUMMARY SOLUTION It is afternoon, A and B are Pemtrus, and C is an Amtru.

S6-3 Three Inhabitants

CONSIDERATIONS

Consider that there are two Pemtrus and one Amtru.

Assume it is afternoon. If so, two of the three are Pemtrus, who have told the truth, and one is an Amtru, who has lied. If so, since A claims that B is a Pemtru and B claims that C is a Pemtru, one of A and B must be the Amtru. It must be A, as stated by C. This means that B and C are the two Pemtrus. However, this means that A, who claims that B is a Pemtru, has spoken truthfully, an impossibility for an Amtru in the afternoon.

Therefore, it must be morning. A and C, who have both lied, are the two Pemtrus, and B, who has told the truth, is the Amtru.

	A	B	C
Amtru	−	+	−
Pemtru	+	−	+

SUMMARY SOLUTION It is morning, A and C are the Pemtrus, and B is the Amtru.

S6-4   Four Inhabitants

CONSIDERATIONS
Consider that two are Amtrus and two are Pemtrus.

Assume it is afternoon. If so, if A is an Amtru, A's statement is false and B is a Pemtru. If so, B's statement is true and C is a Pemtru. If so, C's statement is true and D is a Pemtru. However, D's statement would be false. Therefore, if it is afternoon, A is a Pemtru. If so, B is an Amtru, C is an Amtru, and D is a Pemtru. Again, D's statement would be false, not possible for a Pemtru in the afternoon.

Therefore, it is morning. Assume A is an Amtru. If so, B is an Amtru, C is a Pemtru, and D is an Amtru. However, this would mean only one Pemtru. Therefore, A is a Pemtru, B is a Pemtru, C is an Amtru, and D is an Amtru.

	A	B	C	D
Amtru	−	−	+	+
Pemtru	+	+	−	−

SUMMARY SOLUTION It is morning, A and B are Pemtrus, and C and D are Amtrus.

S6-5   Five Inhabitants

CONSIDERATIONS

Assume it is afternoon, and assume A's statement is true. If so, A is a Pemtru. If so, D, who claims A is an Amtru, must be an Amtru. If it is afternoon, B's statement must be true, and B is a Pemtru. If so, E, who asserts that B is a Pemtru, is also a Pemtru. C, who falsely asserts that D and E belong to the same group, is an Amtru. However, this would mean two Amtrus and three Pemtrus. Since we know there are three Amtrus and two Pemtrus, if it is afternoon and A's statement is not true.

Assume it is afternoon and A's statement is false. If so, A is an Amtru. If so, D, who claims A is an Amtru, is a Pemtru. B must be a Pemtru, as is E. If so, C, who truthfully claims D and E are in the same group, is a Pemtru. However, this would mean four Pemtrus and one Amtru. Therefore, it is not afternoon.

It is morning. Assume B's statement is false. If so, B is a Pemtru. E, who truthfully states B is a Pemtru, is an Amtru. A must be an Amtru. D, who claims A is an Amtru, is an Amtru. C, who truthfully asserts that D and E belong to the same group, is an Amtru. However, this would mean four Amtrus and one Pemtru.

Therefore, since we know it is morning, B's statement is true and B is an Amtru. E, who falsely claims that B is a Pemtru, is a Pemtru. A's statement is true, and A is an Amtru. D, who truthfully asserts that A is an Amtru, is an Amtru. C, who falsely claims that D and E belong to the same group, is a Pemtru.

	A	B	C	D	E
Amtru	+	+	−	+	−
Pemtru	−	−	+	−	+

SUMMARY SOLUTION It is morning, A, B, and D are Amtrus, and C and E are Pemtrus.

S6-6 Four Valley Inhabitants

CONSIDERATIONS

Consider that both groups are represented equally by the four valley inhabitants.

Assume it is afternoon. If so, if C were an Amtru, he would truthfully or falsely assert that B is an Amtru. If C were a Pemtru, again he would truthfully or falsely assert that B is an Amtru. It would be impossible for C to refer to B as a Pemtru. Therefore, since C claims that B is a Pemtru, it can not be afternoon.

It is morning. Whether C is an Amtru or a Pemtru, he has truthfully or falsely stated that B is a Pemtru. From B's statement in the morning, that he and A belong to the same group, we know that B is a Pemtru. (If B were an Amtru, truthfully or falsely he would deny that he and A belong to the same group.)

For the same reason, from A's statement, A is a Pemtru and D could be an Amtru or a Pemtru. However, since both groups are represented equally, D and C must both be Amtrus.

	A	B	C	D
Amtru	–	–	+	+
Pemtru	+	+	–	–

SUMMARY SOLUTION It is morning, A and B are Pemtrus, and C and D are Amtrus.

CONSIDERATIONS

Assume it is afternoon. If so, from A's statement we can conclude that A is an Amtru, as a Pemtru in the afternoon could not refer to another valley inhabitant as a Pemtru. If it is afternoon, C must be a Pemtru, as an Amtru would be truthfully referred to as such by A. However, B's statement that he and C are not both Amtrus would be true, which is not a possible statement in the afternoon.

Therefore, it is morning. A is either a Pemtru who has spoken truthfully or falsely about C, or an Amtru who has spoken falsely in a statement referring to another Amtru (if C were a Pemtru, A would truthfully say so).

Assume A is a Pemtru. If so, if C is a Pemtru, C's statement, which refers to A, must be true: A would say that B is an Amtru. However, as a Pemtru in the morning, A's reference to B as an Amtru must be false. Therefore, B must be a Pemtru. However, this is a contradiction, as A's reference to another Pemtru in the morning must be true.

Therefore, if A is a Pemtru, C must be an Amtru. If so, again, C's statement would be true: A would falsely say that B is an Amtru, which leads to the same contradiction as in the previous paragraph.

Therefore, A and C are both Amtrus. C's statement referring to A must be false: A would not say that B is an Amtru. B must be an Amtru who has spoken falsely about another Amtru.

	A	B	C
Amtru	+	+	+
Pemtru	–	–	–

SUMMARY SOLUTION It is morning, and A, B, and C are Amtrus.

S6-8   Does C Live on the Hill?

CONSIDERATIONS

Consider that the hill inhabitant will speak the truth only if none of the other speakers are truthful. Otherwise, he will lie. Also consider that it is afternoon.

If C is the hill inhabitant as claimed, B has spoken falsely and, therefore, must be an Amtru. A, who truthfully confirms this, must be a Pemtru. As the hill inhabitant, C could not have spoken truthfully. Therefore, C is not the hill inhabitant.

C, who has spoken falsely, must be an Amtru. B, who falsely claims C is a Pemtru, could be an Amtru or the hill inhabitant. If B is the hill inhabitant, A's statement is false and A is an Amtru. D, who falsely states that A is a Pemtru, must be an Amtru. Therefore, since A, C, and D all make false statements, B, if the hill inhabitant, would speak truthfully. Since B falsely claims C to be a Pemtru, B is not the hill inhabitant.

Therefore, the hill inhabitant must be A or D. Assume D is the hill inhabitant. If so, since A truthfully states that B is an Amtru, he is a Pemtru. If D is the hill inhabitant, his statement would be false. However, it is not. Therefore, A, who has spoken truthfully, is the hill inhabitant. B, C, and D have spoken falsely; all three are Amtrus.

	A	B	C	D
Amtru	−	+	+	+
Pemtru	−	−	−	−
Hill	+	−	−	−

SUMMARY SOLUTION   A is the hill inhabitant, and B, C, and D are Amtrus.

S6-9   One from the Hill

CONSIDERATIONS

Consider that the hill inhabitant will speak the truth only if none of the other speakers are truthful. Otherwise, he will lie.

Assume that A is the hill inhabitant. If so, if it is morning, D's statement is true, and A's statement about D is also true. But a hill inhabitant lies if others speak the truth, so if A is the hill inhabitant, it must be afternoon. If so, B's statement is true, so A's statement must be false. This means D is a Pemtru and his statement is true. But since C's statement is not true, C is an Amtru, which contradicts D's statement. Therefore, A does not live on the hill.

Assume that B is the hill inhabitant. If so, B's statement about C must be true. But C's statement is also true. Therefore, B is not the hill inhabitant.

Assume that C is the hill inhabitant. If so, C's statement is true, and D's statement is true too. Therefore, C is not the hill inhabitant.

Therefore, D lives on the hill. B's statement is true, so D's statement must be false. Since C's statement is false, from D's false statement C must be an Amtru, and it must be afternoon. So B is a Pemtru, and A, whose statement is true, is also an Pemtru.

	A	B	C	D
Amtru	–	–	+	–
Pemtru	+	+	–	–
Hill	–	–	–	+

SUMMARY SOLUTION It is afternoon, D is the hill inhabitant, A and B are Pemtrus, and C is an Amtru.

Index

Page key: puzzle, *clues*, **solution**